Drawings from the Clark Art Institute · The Plates

Frontispiece, Volume II (overleaf)
Peter Paul Rubens. *Portrait of Thomas Howard, Earl of Arundel*
18¼ x 14″ Catalogue number 22

Drawings from the Clark Art Institute

*A Catalogue Raisonné of the Robert Sterling Clark
Collection of European and American Drawings,
Sixteenth through Nineteenth Centuries, at the
Sterling and Francine Clark Art Institute, Williamstown*

*by Egbert Haverkamp-Begemann,
Standish D. Lawder, and Charles W. Talbot, Jr.*

Volume Two: The Plates

New Haven and London: Yale University Press, 1964

Copyright © 1964 by Yale University.

Designed by Alvin Eisenman,
set in Garamond type,
and printed in the United States of America by
The Carl Purington Rollins Printing-Office of
the Yale University Press.
Color plates and printing by
The Meriden Gravure Company.

Library of Congress catalog card number: 64–20922

Published with assistance from
the Sterling and Francine Clark Art Institute,
Williamstown, Massachusetts.

List of Plates

List of Plates

Plate 43. Pierre Paul Prud'hon. *'La Source'*. Catalogue number 45.

Plate 44. Jean-Baptiste Greuze. *The Motherly Reprimand*. Catalogue number 37.

Plate 45. Hubert Robert. *Fishermen Drawing their Net*. Catalogue number 46.

Plate 46. Étienne Aubry. *Mother and Children*. Catalogue number 32.

Plate 47. Moreau le Jeune. *Céphise with Dog*. Catalogue number 43.

Eighteenth Century · Italy

Plate 48 (Color). Giovanni Battista Tiepolo. *Hagar and Ishmael in the Wilderness*. Catalogue number 55.

Plate 49. Giovanni Battista Tiepolo. *The Liberation of St. Peter*. Catalogue number 56.

Plate 50. Giovanni Battista Tiepolo. *The Annunciation*. Catalogue number 57.

Plate 51. Giovanni Battista Tiepolo. *The Rest on the Flight into Egypt*. Catalogue number 58.

Plate 52. Giovanni Battista Tiepolo. *The Flight into Egypt*. Catalogue number 59.

Plate 53. Giovanni Domenico Tiepolo. *Burial of Saint Anne*. Catalogue number 60.

Plate 54. Giovanni Domenico Tiepolo. *Nebuchadnezzar Returning from the Wilderness to His Palace*, Detail. Catalogue number 63.

Plate 55. Giovanni Domenico Tiepolo. *Nebuchadnezzar Returning from the Wilderness to His Palace*. Catalogue number 63.

Plate 56. Giovanni Domenico Tiepolo. *A Group Astonished by a Girl*. Catalogue number 62.

Plate 57. Giovanni Domenico Tiepolo. *The Liberation of St. Peter and St. John from Prison*. Catalogue number 61.

Plate 58. Giovanni Domenico Tiepolo. *A Disputation Between Kings and Priests*, Detail. Catalogue number 64.

Plate 59. Giovanni Domenico Tiepolo. *A Disputation Between Kings and Priests*. Catalogue number 64.

Nineteenth Century · England

Plate 60. Sir David Wilkie. *Three Greek Sisters of Therapia*. Catalogue number 73.

Plate 61. William Turner. *Lynmouth, Devonshire*. Catalogue number 69.

Plate 62 (Color). William Turner. *Brunnen, from the Lake of Lucerne*. Catalogue number 71.

Plate 63. William Turner. *Clifton, Gloucestershire*. Catalogue number 70.

Plate 64. Frederick Leighton. *Portrait of Miss Dorothy Dene*. Catalogue number 68.

Plate 65. Frederick Leighton. *Study for 'Whispers'*. Catalogue number 67.

Nineteenth Century · France

Plate 66. Wille Fils. *Young Woman at a Window*. Catalogue number 302.

Plate 67. Louis-Léopold Boilly. *Woman with Child and Dog*. Catalogue number 80.

Plate 68. Jean-François Bosio. *'Un salon parisien en 1801'*. Catalogue number 83.

Plate 69. Eugène Delacroix. *Studies of Horses*. Catalogue number 169.

Plate 70. Eugène Delacroix. *Studies of a Crouching Tiger*. Catalogue number 170.

Plate 71. Eugène Delacroix. *Two Studies of a Lioness*. Catalogue number 176.

Plate 72. Eugène Delacroix. *Abd-er-Rahman II, Sultan of Morocco*. Catalogue number 174.

Plate 73. Eugène Delacroix. *Two Seated Moors in Conversation and Studies of an Arm, Leg, and Hands*. Catalogue number 171.

Plate 74. Eugène Delacroix. *Head of a Woman*. Catalogue number 172.

Plate 75 (Color). Eugène Delacroix. *Nude Woman*. Catalogue number 175.

Plate 76. Eugène Delacroix. *Winter Landscape*. Catalogue number 173.

Plate 77. Alexandre-Gabriel Decamps. *Old Woman Drinking*. Catalogue number 146.

Plate 78. Alexandre-Gabriel Decamps. *Turkish Woman Smoking*. Catalogue number 143.

Plate 79. Alexandre-Gabriel Decamps. *Caravan Halted at an Oasis*. Catalogue number 144.

Plate 80. Alexandre-Gabriel Decamps. *A Boy Leading His Animal Troupe*. Catalogue number 147.

Plate 81. Alexandre-Gabriel Decamps. *Peasant Woman Seen from the Back*. Catalogue number 145.

Plate 82. Charles Jacque. *An Infantryman*. Catalogue number 224.

Plate 83. Charles Jacque. *Pierrette Lorrain*. Catalogue number 225.

Plate 84. David d'Angers. *Profile of a Gentleman*. Catalogue number 142.

Plate 85. Théodore Chassériau. *A Saint Receiving the Christ Child from the Virgin Mary*. Catalogue number 86.

Sixteenth and Seventeenth Centuries · Various Countries

Plate 1
Jean Bourdichon. *Saint Mark*
7 ¹¹⁄₁₆ x 5 ¹¹⁄₁₆″ Catalogue number 1

Plate 2
Albrecht Dürer. *Head of a Young Man*
8¾ x 7⅛″ Catalogue number 2

Plate 3
Albrecht Dürer. *Sketches of Animals and Landscapes*, Detail.
Catalogue number 3

Plate 4
Albrecht Dürer. *Sketches of Animals and Landscapes,* Detail
Catalogue number 3

Plate 5 Albrecht Dürer.
Sketches of Animals and Landscapes
10⁷/₁₆ x 15⅝" Catalogue number 3

Plate 6
Attributed to Hans Holbein the Younger. *Portrait of a Man*
Diameter 12¾″ Catalogue number 4

Plate 7
Perugino. *Kneeling Figure and Two Heads*
8⅝ x 5⅜″ Catalogue number 8

Plate 8
After Perugino. *Mercury*
9¼ x 7³⁄₁₆″ Catalogue number 10

Plate 9
Follower of Leonardo da Vinci. *Head of a Woman*
5 ⅞ x 4 ⅞″ Catalogue number 7

Plate 10
Timoteo Viti. *Study of a Nude*
9⅜ x 6½″ Catalogue number 12

Plate 11
After Perugino. *Baptism of Christ*
11⁵⁄₁₆ x 7⅝″ Catalogue number 9

Plate 12
Fra Bartolommeo. *Madonna and Child with Angels*
7 7/16 x 6 3/16″ Catalogue number 6

Plate 13
Fra Bartolommeo. *Fragment of a Lamentation* (reverse of Plate 12)
7 7/16 x 6 3/16″ Catalogue number 6

Plate 14
Sixteenth-Century Venetian. *Head of a Girl*
9⅛ x 7¹⁄₁₆″ Catalogue number 14

Plate 15
Andrea del Sarto. *Study of Drapery*
10¼ x 13⁷⁄₁₆″ Catalogue number 5

Plate 16
School of Titian.
Venus Bathing, with Cupid and Psyche
10⁹⁄₁₆ x 15⅛″ Catalogue number 11

Plate 17
School of Pietro da Cortona. *Head and Shoulders of a Woman*
9⅞ x 8″ Catalogue number 15

Plate 18
Attributed to Pieter Molijn. *Village Road*
5 ¹⁵⁄₁₆ x 7 ½″ Catalogue number 16

Plate 19
Willem van de Velde the Younger. *Dutch Men-of-War*
6 ³⁄₁₆ x 13 ⁷⁄₁₆″ Catalogue number 23

Plate 20
School of Anthony van Dyck. *View on the Bank of a River*
11 ¼ x 7 ⁹⁄₁₆″ Catalogue number 24

Plate 21
Rembrandt. *Farm under Trees*
4⁷⁄₁₆ x 6½″ Catalogue number 17

Plate 22
Rembrandt. *Christ Finding the Apostles Asleep*
7¼ x 11″ Catalogue number 18

Plate 24
Peter Paul Rubens. *Hercules Strangling the Nemean Lion*
12½ x 19 1/16″ Catalogue number 20

Plate 23
Peter Paul Rubens. *Hercules Strangling the Nemean Lion*, Detail
Catalogue number 20

Plate 26
Peter Paul Rubens. *Venus and Cupid*
5⅛ x 4⅜" Catalogue number 21

Plate 25
Peter Paul Rubens. *Portrait of Thomas Howard, Earl of Arundel*, Detail
Catalogue number 22

Eighteenth Century · Various Countries

Plate 27
Thomas Gainsborough. *Herdsman and Cattle*
8⅞ x 12¼" Catalogue number 26

Plate 28
Thomas Gainsborough. *Landscape with View over a Distant Plain*
8½ x 12⅟₁₆″ Catalogue number 27

Plate 29
William Payne. *A Cottage at Wyesham*
9 15/16 x 16 1/16″ Catalogue number 29

Plate 30
Thomas Rowlandson. *Rustic Lovers*
6⅜ x 5⅛″ Catalogue number 30

Plate 31
Thomas Rowlandson. *The Fine White Cauliflower*
7³⁄₁₆ x 5¼″ Catalogue number 31

Plate 32
Antoine Watteau.
Two Studies of a Woman with a Fan, Detail
Catalogue number 51

Plate 33
Antoine Watteau. *Two Studies of a Woman with a Fan*
9¾ x 13¹⁵⁄₁₆″ Catalogue number 51

Plate 34
Antoine Watteau. *Woman in Black*
7¾ x 7¹⁄₁₆″ Catalogue number 52

Plate 35
François Boucher. *Head of a Girl*
6⁷⁄₁₆ x 4⁷⁄₈″ Catalogue number 34

Plate 36
Jean-Honoré Fragonard. *'Les Jets d'eau'*
10⁷⁄₁₆ x 15⅛″ Catalogue number 36

Plate 37
Louis-René Boquet. *Costume Design*
9⁷⁄₁₆ x 6″ Catalogue number 33

Plate 38
Claude Hoin. *The Love Letter*
12⁷⁄₈ x 9¹¹⁄₁₆″ Catalogue number 39

Plate 39
Pierre Lelu. *Well at Mâcon*
7 11/16 x 9 9/16″ Catalogue number 41

Plate 40
Constantin d'Aix. *A Ruin on a Hillside*
10⅞₁₆ x 14¹⁵⁄₁₆″ Catalogue number 35

Plate 41
Nicolas-Antoine Taunay. *Battle of Fleurus*
4⁵⁄₁₆ x 6⅛″ Catalogue number 49

Plate 42
Moreau l'Aîné. *A Farmyard*
11 x 9⅜″ Catalogue number 42

Plate 43
Pierre Paul Prud'hon. *'La Source'*
21 ³⁄₁₆ x 15 ⁵⁄₁₆" Catalogue number 45

Plate 44
Jean-Baptiste Greuze. *The Motherly Reprimand*
18 x 13½" Catalogue number 37

Plate 45
Hubert Robert. *Fishermen Drawing their Net*
7 13/16 x 12 5/16" Catalogue number 46

Plate 46
Étienne Aubry. *Mother and Children*
12 x 16⅛" Catalogue number 32

Plate 47
Moreau le Jeune. *Céphise with Dog*
12⅜ x 9¼″ Catalogue number 43

Plate 48
Giovanni Battista Tiepolo.
Hagar and Ishmael in the Wilderness
16½ x 11⅛″ Catalogue number 55

Plate 49
Giovanni Battista Tiepolo.
The Liberation of St. Peter
17⅛ x 11⁷⁄₁₆″ Catalogue number 56

Plate 50
Giovanni Battista Tiepolo.
The Annunciation
17 x 11¾" Catalogue number 57

Plate 51
Giovanni Battista Tiepolo.
The Rest on the Flight into Egypt
12 x 8⅞″ Catalogue number 58

Plate 52
Giovanni Battista Tiepolo.
The Flight into Egypt
9⅝ x 8¹/₁₆″ Catalogue number

Plate 53
Giovanni Domenico Tiepolo. *Burial of Saint Anne*
18⅞ x 14⅞″ Catalogue number 60

Plate 54
Giovanni Domenico Tiepolo. *Nebuchadnezzar Returning from the Wilderness to His Palace*, Detail
Catalogue number 63

Plate 55
Giovanni Domenico Tiepolo.
Nebuchadnezzar Returning from the Wilderness to His Palace
19⁵⁄₁₆ x 15⅛″ Catalogue number 63

Plate 58
Giovanni Domenico Tiepolo. *A Disputation Between Kings and Priests,* Detail
Catalogue number 64

Plate 56
Giovanni Domenico Tiepolo. *A Group Astonished by a Girl*
19⁹⁄₁₆ x 15⅛″ Catalogue number 62

Plate 57
Giovanni Domenico Tiepolo. *The Liberation of St. Peter and St. John from Prison*
19⁹⁄₁₆ x 15¹⁄₁₆″ Catalogue number 61

Plate 59
Giovanni Domenico Tiepolo. *A Disputation Between Kings and Priests*
19⅜ x 15¹⁄₁₆″ Catalogue number 64

Nineteenth Century · England

Plate 60
Sir David Wilkie. *Three Greek Sisters of Therapia*
9¾ x 14″ Catalogue number 73

Plate 61
William Turner. *Lynmouth, Devonshire*
8 13⁄16 x 12 7⁄8″ Catalogue number 69

Plate 62
William Turner. *Brunnen, from the Lake of Lucerne*
11⅝ x 18¹³⁄₁₆″ Catalogue number 71

Plate 63
William Turner. *Clifton, Gloucestershire*
8¾ x 12⁷⁄₁₆″ Catalogue number 70

Plate 64
Frederick Leighton. *Portrait of Miss Dorothy Dene*
11½ x 8¾" Catalogue number 68

Plate 65
Frederick Leighton. *Study for 'Whispers'*
13 x 9¼" Catalogue number 67

Nineteenth Century · France

Plate 66
Wille Fils. *Young Woman at a Window*
14⅝ x 10¾″ Catalogue number 302

Plate 67
Louis-Léopold Boilly. *Woman with Child and Dog*
12⅞ x 9¾″ Catalogue number 80

Plate 68
Jean-François Bosio. *'Un salon parisien en 1801'*
14⅝ x 19⅝" Catalogue number 83

10 aout 1832.

E.D

Plate 69
Eugène Delacroix. *Studies of Horses*
8¼ x 10⅞″ Catalogue number 169

Plate 70
Eugène Delacroix. *Studies of a Crouching Tiger*
5 9/16 x 8 7/8" Catalogue number 170

Plate 71
Eugène Delacroix. *Two Studies of a Lioness*
5 ³⁄₁₆ x 7 ⁵⁄₈″ Catalogue number 176

Plate 72
Eugène Delacroix. *Abd-er-Rahman II, Sultan of Morocco*
9⁹⁄₁₆ x 6³⁄₁₆" Catalogue number 174

Plate 73
Eugène Delacroix. *Two Seated Moors in Conversation and Studies of an Arm, Leg, and Hands*
7³⁄₁₆ x 11⅛″ Catalogue number 171

Plate 74
Eugène Delacroix. *Head of a Woman*
8⅝ x 8⅝" Catalogue number 172

Plate 75
Eugène Delacroix. *Nude Woman*
6¹¹⁄₁₆ x 4⅛″ Catalogue number 175

Plate 76
Eugène Delacroix. *Winter Landscape*
10⅜ x 15¹⁄₁₆″ Catalogue number 173

Plate 77
Alexandre-Gabriel Decamps. *Old Woman Drinking*
8¾ x 7⅟₁₆″ Catalogue number 146

Plate 78
Alexandre-Gabriel Decamps. *Turkish Woman Smoking*
5 1³⁄₁₆ x 4³⁄₁₆″ Catalogue number 143

Plate 79
Alexandre-Gabriel Decamps.
Caravan Halted at an Oasis
8½ x 11⁵⁄₁₆″ Catalogue number 144

Plate 80
Alexandre-Gabriel Decamps.
A Boy Leading His Animal Troupe
6½ x 9¹⁵⁄₁₆″ Catalogue number 147

Plate 81
Alexandre-Gabriel Decamps.
Peasant Woman Seen from the Back
10⁵⁄₁₆ x 6⅞″ Catalogue number 145

Plate 82
Charles Jacque. *An Infantryman*
4¼ x 3⅜" Catalogue number 224

Plate 83
Charles Jacque. *Pierrette Lorrain*
6¹⁄₁₆ x 4⁵⁄₁₆" Catalogue number 225

Plate 84
David d'Angers. *Profile of a Gentleman*
4¹³⁄₁₆ x 4¼" Catalogue number 142

Plate 85
Théodore Chassériau.
A Saint Receiving the Christ Child from the Virgin Mary
16⁵⁄₁₆ x 12⅞" Catalogue number 86

Plate 86
Ingres. *Study for 'L'Âge d'or'*
13⅝ x 6⅝″ Catalogue number 222

Plate 87
Honoré Daumier. *Two Colleagues*
9¼ x 7⁵⁄₁₆" Catalogue number 119

Plate 88
Honoré Daumier.
Three Lawyers
12 15/16 x 9¾"
Catalogue number 118

Plate 89
Honoré Daumier. *Three Lawyers*, Detail
Catalogue number 118

Plate 90
Honoré Daumier. *The Song*
9⁵⁄₁₆ x 10⁷⁄₁₆″ Catalogue number 120

Plate 91
Paul Gavarni. *The Poacher*
7⅞ x 5 ¹³⁄₁₆″ Catalogue number 202

Plate 92
Henry Monnier. *M. Prud'homme and a Friend*
11 ¹⁵⁄₁₆ x 8⅜″ Catalogue number 262

Plate 93
Jean-Léon Gérôme. *Two Soldiers Playing Checkers*
7⅜ x 10¹³⁄₁₆″ Catalogue number 203

Plate 94
Charles Meryon. *Old House in Bourges: 'La Maison du Musicien'*
10⅜ x 5¹³⁄₁₆″ Catalogue number 248

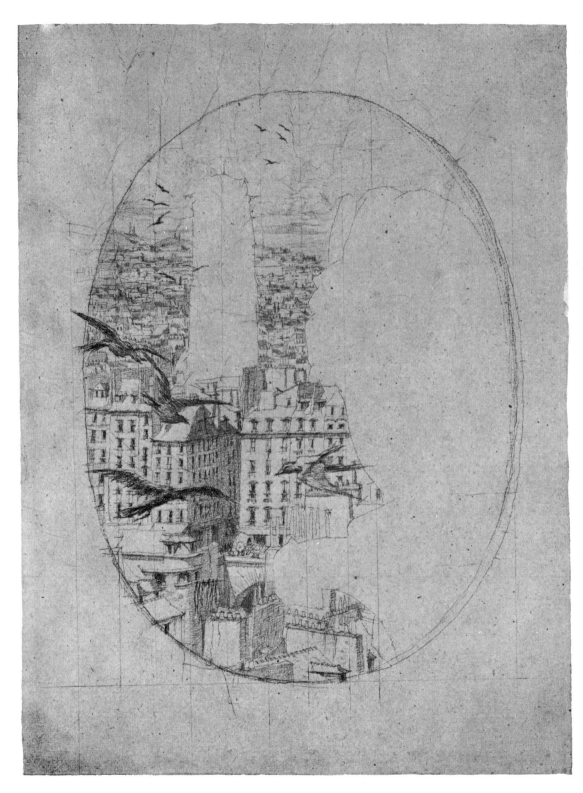

Plate 95
Charles Meryon. *Study for 'Le Stryge': The City and the Birds*
7 13/16 x 5 7/8″ Catalogue number 251

Plate 96
Charles Meryon. *Study for 'Le Stryge': The Chimera and the Tower of Saint Jacques*
7 7/8 x 4 7/8″ Catalogue number 250

Plate 97
Charles Meryon. *A Chimera of Notre Dame, Paris*
8⅛ x 4⅞″ Catalogue number 252

Plate 98
Charles Meryon. *Le Pont-au-Change, Paris*
6¹³⁄₁₆ x 13⅛" Catalogue number 253

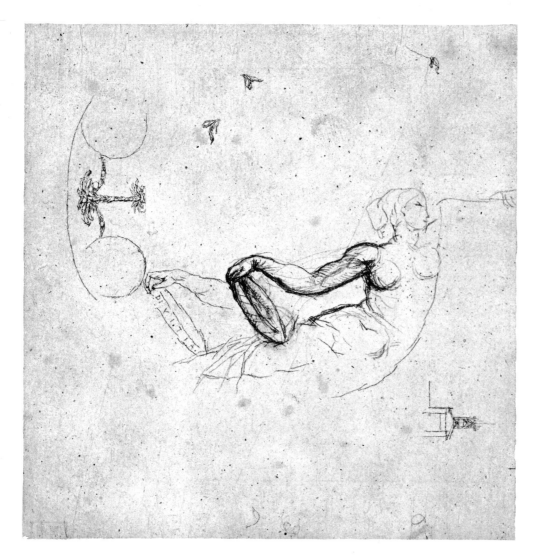

Plate 99
Charles Meryon.
Studies for 'View of San Francisco':
Figure of Abundance and Architectural Details
5 ⅜ x 5 ⁵⁄₁₆″ Catalogue number 256

Plate 100
Charles Meryon.
Studies for 'View of San Francisco': Horses and Riders
3 ¹⁵⁄₁₆ x 2 ⅜″ Catalogue number 257

Plate 101
Charles Meryon. *Study for 'L'Arche du Pont Notre-Dame'*
6¹³⁄₁₆ x 8¼″ Catalogue number 249

Plate 102
Charles Meryon. *Anthropomorphic Cloud Studies (Second Version)*
3 7/8 x 7 15/16″ Catalogue number 255

Plate 103
Charles Meryon. *Anthropomorphic Cloud Studies (First Version)*
3 1/8 x 7 15/16″ Catalogue number 254

Plate 104
Constantin Guys. *Amelia Masi*
11 13/16 x 8 7/8″ Catalogue number 207

Plate 105
Constantin Guys. *A Grisette*
7 ³⁄₁₆ x 5 ³⁄₁₆″ Catalogue number 209

Plate 106
Constantin Guys. *Groom with Three Horses*
6⅞ x 8½″ Catalogue number 208

Plate 107
Constantin Guys. *The Loge of the French Empress*
9 x 13¾₁₆″ Catalogue number 211

Plate 108
Constantin Guys. *Lady in an Evening Gown*
8¹⁵⁄₁₆ x 6⅛″ Catalogue number 210

Plate 109
Jean-François Millet. *Study of a Kneeling Woman*
6½ x 4¾″ Catalogue number 258

Plate 110
Corot. *The Farewell*
9⅑₁₆ x 6⅛″ Catalogue number 115

Plate III
Théodore Rousseau. *River in a Valley*
7⅛ x 10⅝" Catalogue number 289

Plate 112
Théodore Rousseau. *The Edge of the Lake*
5⅛ x 11″ Catalogue number 288

Plate 113
Diaz de la Peña. *Landscape*
6 x 11″ Catalogue number 181

Plate 115
Constant Troyon. *Entrance into the Forest*
7 ⁹⁄₁₆ x 5 ⅜″ Catalogue number 299

Plate 114
Jules Dupré. *The Watering Place*
11 ⅞ x 9 ⁷⁄₁₆″ Catalogue number 183

Plate 116
Henri Harpignies. *River Landscape*
9¹¹⁄₁₆ x 8⁹⁄₁₆″ Catalogue number 216

Plate 117
Auguste Raffet. *Prussian Infantry*
16½ x 10¼″ Catalogue number 279

Plate 118
William Bouguereau. *A Nude Study for Venus*
18 3/16 x 11 15/16" Catalogue number 84

.68

G. Courbet,

Plate 120
Rosa Bonheur. *Bull Resting*
11¾ x 17¼″ Catalogue number 81

Plate 119
Gustave Courbet. *Alms from a Beggar, at Ornans*
11¼ x 8¹³⁄₁₆″ Catalogue number 116

Plate 121
Ernest Meissonier. *Polichinelle*
7⅜ x 4¾″ Catalogue number 247

Plate 122
Paul Delamain. *Head and Forequarters of a Mounted Horse*
9⅛ x 6⁹⁄₁₆″ Catalogue number 180

Plate 123
Nadar. *Émile Augier*
12 x 9³⁄₁₆″ Catalogue number 268

Plate 124
Édouard de Beaumont. *A Man Ladies Notice*
9 1/16 x 8 1/16″ Catalogue number 78

Plate 125
Abel Damourette. *Two Ladies and a Gentleman*
10 5/8 x 8 9/16″ Catalogue number 117

Plate 126
Jules David. *Fashion Drawing (No. 18)*
11 7/8 x 9 1/4″ Catalogue number 138

Plate 127
Édouard Manet. *Woman Writing*
5⁹⁄₁₆ x 6¼″ Catalogue number 243

Plate 128
Édouard Manet. *Woman in a Large Hat*
7 x 4 15/16″ Catalogue number 244

Plate 129
Paul Adolphe Rajon. *Portrait of Pablo Sarasate*
10⅝ x 8⁷⁄₁₆″ Catalogue number 280

Plate 130
Jean-Baptiste Carpeaux. *Portrait of a Woman*
7⅞ x 5⅞″ Catalogue number 85

Plate 131
Claude Monet. *View of Rouen*
12⅞ x 19¹³⁄₁₆″ Catalogue number 259

Plate 132
Henri Fantin-Latour. *Mary Magdalene*
8¹³⁄₁₆ x 6¹³⁄₁₆″ Catalogue number 184

Plate 133
Berthe Morisot. *Marthe Givaudan*
10½ x 9″ Catalogue number 267

Plate 134
Berthe Morisot. *Harbor Scene*
8⅛ x 10½" Catalogue number 266

Plate 135
Puvis de Chavannes. *Study of a Woman's Head*
6¾ x 5¼" Catalogue number 270

Plate 136
Puvis de Chavannes. *Kneeling Youth*
12 11/16 x 9 1/2″ Catalogue number 273

Plate 137
Puvis de Chavannes. *Standing Woman with a Pitcher*
9 7/16 x 4 1/2″ Catalogue number 272

R.P.C.

Plate 138
Puvis de Chavannes.
Woman with a Bowl and a Sheaf of Grain
12⅝₁₆ x 8¹¹⁄₁₆″ Catalogue number 271

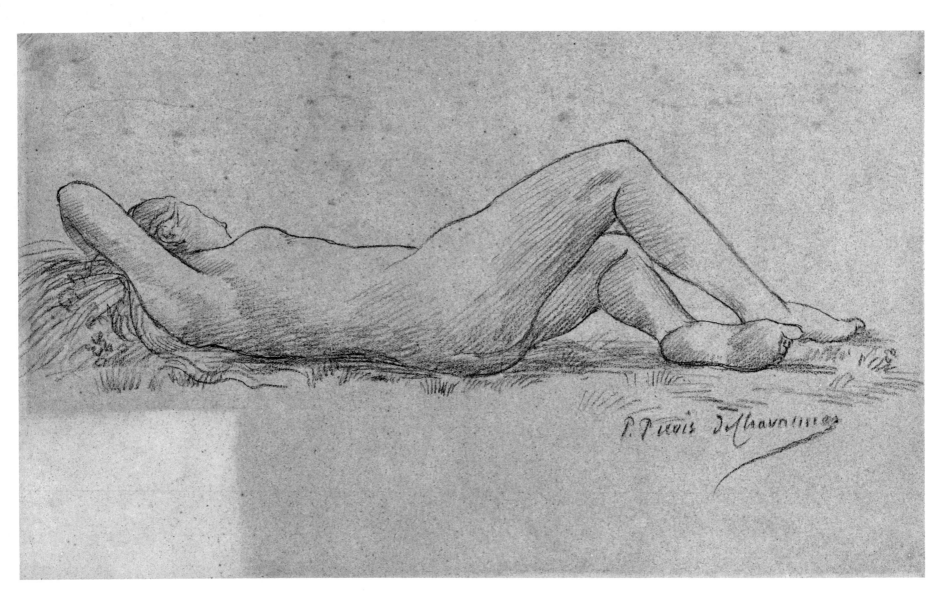

Plate 139
Puvis de Chavannes. *Study for a Bather*
7 ½ x 12 ⅜″ Catalogue number 275

Plate 140
Puvis de Chavannes. *Study for 'La Veillée de Ste. Geneviève'*
17⅛ x 7⅛″ Catalogue number 276

Plate 141
Puvis de Chavannes. *Study for Personification of the Saône*
9⁵⁄₁₆ x 4¹³⁄₁₆″ Catalogue number 274

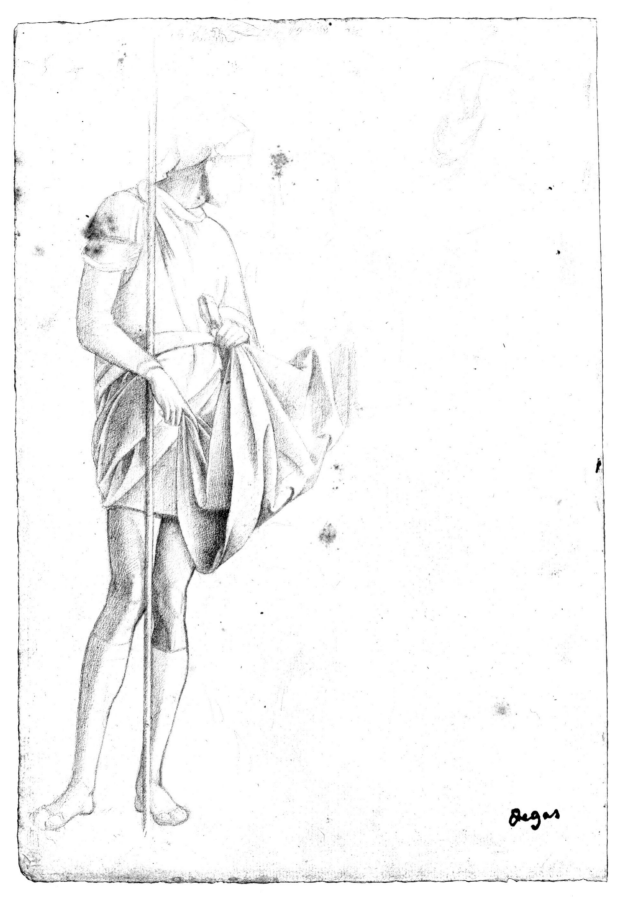

Plate 142
Edgar Degas. *Roman Soldier, after Mantegna*
12⅛ x 8½" Catalogue number 148

Plate 143
Edgar Degas. *Two Portrait Studies of a Man*
17⅝ x 11¼" Catalogue number 149

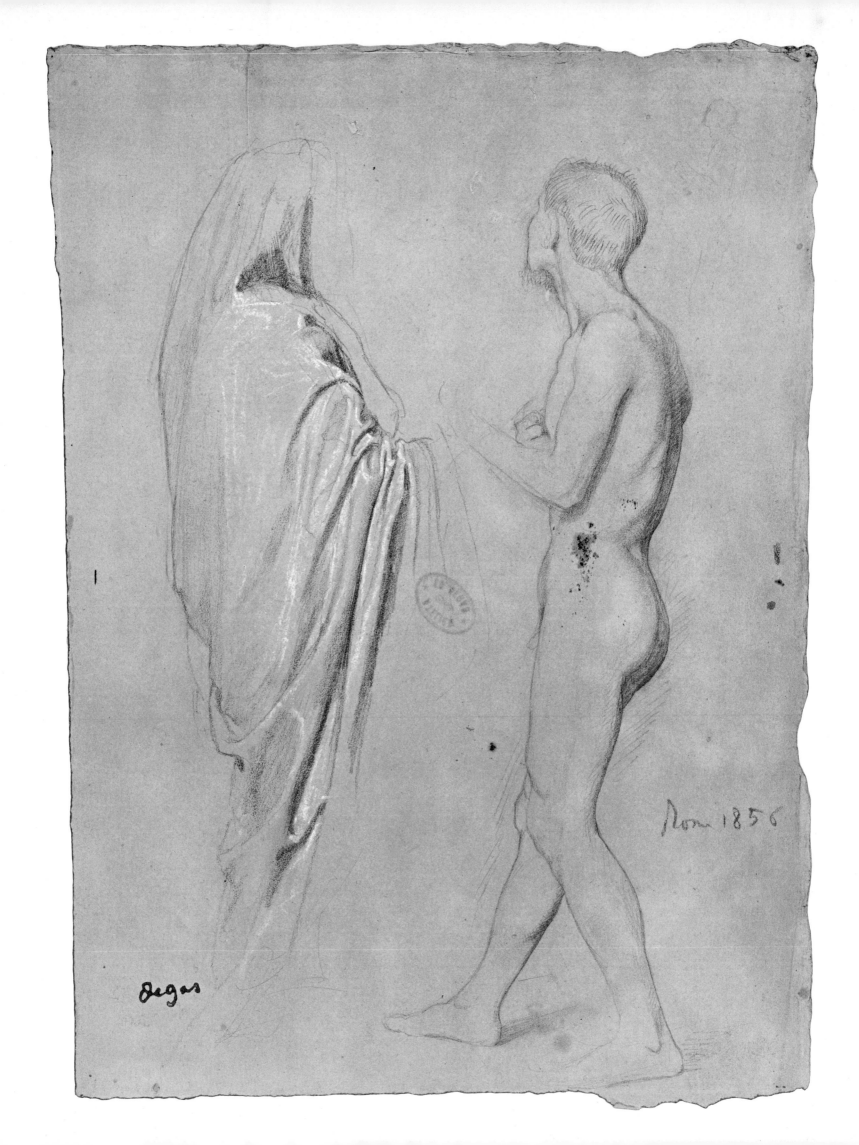

Rom 1856

Degas

Plate 145
Edgar Degas. *At the Races*
13¾ x 19″ Catalogue number 152

Plate 144
Edgar Degas. *Study for 'Dante and Virgil'*
12⅛ x 8¹³⁄₁₆″ Catalogue number 150

Plate 146
Edgar Degas. *Study of an Arm*
12⅛ x 6¼" Catalogue number 153

Plate 147
Edgar Degas. *Old Man Seated*
10⅞₆ x 7¹³⁄₁₆" Catalogue number 154

Plate 148
Edgar Degas. *Standing Nude*
11½ x 8⁹⁄₁₆" Catalogue number 151

Degas

Plate 149
Edgar Degas. *Study of Drapery*
10⅜ x 7⅝″ Catalogue number 155

Plate 150
Edgar Degas. *Portrait of a Man*
13¾ x 10½″ Catalogue number 163

Plate 151
Edgar Degas. *Studies of Horses*
9⅛ x 14″ Catalogue number 158

Plate 152
Edgar Degas. *Man Riding*
9⅝ x 13½″ Catalogue number 161

degas
1863

Mme Jules Bertin

Plate 153
Edgar Degas.
Madame Julie Burtin
12⅛ x 8½″
Catalogue number 156

Plate 154
Edgar Degas. *Study for 'Steeplechase –*
The Fallen Jockey': The Jockey
12⅜ x 17⅝″ Catalogue number 160

Plate 155
Edgar Degas. *Dead Fox*
8⅛ x 10⅞″ Catalogue number 157

Degas

ph: 2380

Plate 156
Edgar Degas. *Study for 'Steeplechase – The Fallen Jockey': The Horse*
9⅛ x 14" Catalogue number 159

Plate 157
Edgar Degas. *Racehorse*
11¼ x 14¾" Catalogue number 164

Plate 158
Edgar Degas. *Two Horses, One Nuzzling the Other*
9½ x 12⁷⁄₁₆" Catalogue number 165

Plate 159
Edgar Degas. *Jockey on a Rearing Horse*
9¼ x 14¼" Catalogue number 166

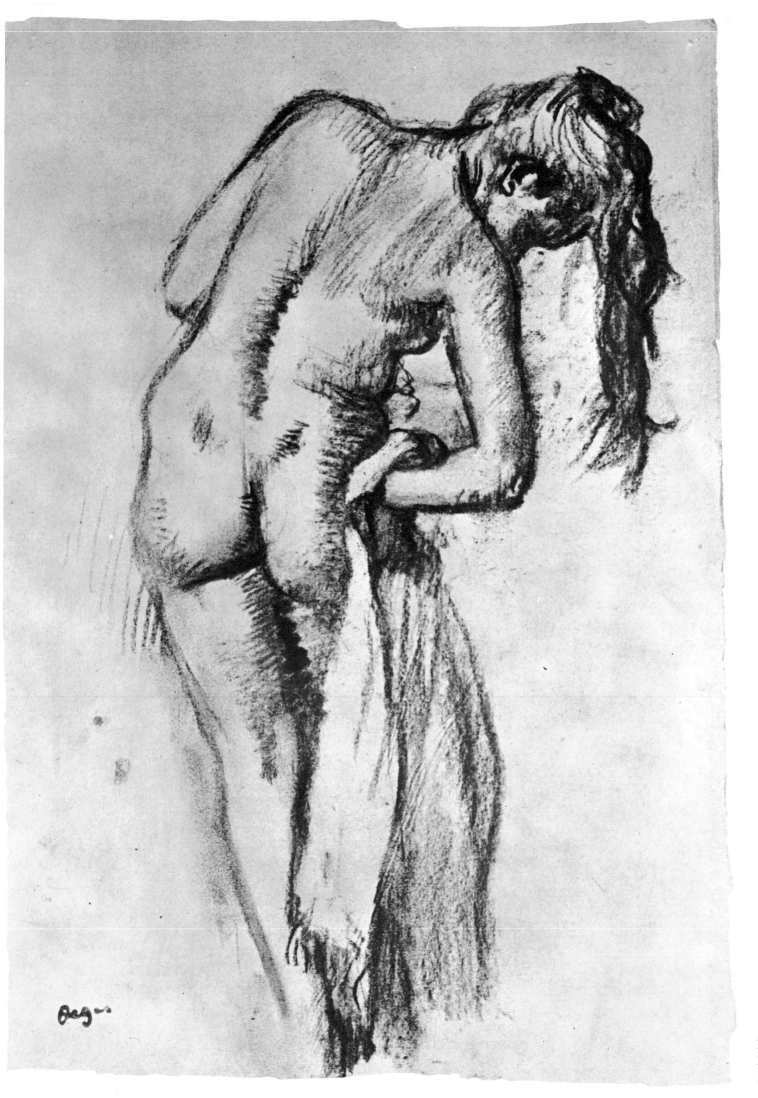

Plate 160
Edgar Degas. *After the Bath*
13⅞ x 10″ Catalogue number 168

Plate 161
Edgar Degas.
Woman Standing in a Bath Tub
17¼ x 12″ Catalogue number 167

Degas

Plate 162
Edgar Degas. *Violinist*
17⅛ x 12⅛″
Catalogue number 162

Plate 163
Jean-Louis Forain.
Avenue in the 'Bois de Boulogne'
8³⁄₁₆ x 5³⁄₁₆″ Catalogue number 186

Plate 164
Jean-Louis Forain. *Owner and Jockey*
8⅛ x 5¼″ Catalogue number 185

Plate 165
Jean-Louis Forain. *Idyll*
8¹⁄₁₆ x 5¼″ Catalogue number 189

Plate 166
Jean-Louis Forain. *Flirts and Follower*
8³⁄₁₆ x 5¼″ Catalogue number 187

Plate 167
Jean-Louis Forain. *Equestrienne*
10⅜ x 13⅛″ Catalogue number 196

foran

17-42

Plate 168
Jean-Louis Forain.
Ballet Dancer Seen from the Back
18¹⁵⁄₁₆ x 12¹⁵⁄₁₆″ Catalogue number 198

Plate 169
Paul Helleu. *Studies of Heads*
10½ x 15¹¹⁄₁₆″ Catalogue number 221

Plate 170
Jules Chéret. *Clown Seated on a Stool, Holding her Mask*
15 9/16 x 9 9/16" Catalogue number 92

Plate 171
Jules Chéret. *Woman Leaning on the Back of a Chair, Facing to the Left*
15 3/4 x 9 7/8" Catalogue number 106

Plate 172
Jules Chéret. *Léonie Laporte as a Bacchante*
12 7/16 x 9 1/2" Catalogue number 112

Plate 173
Jules Chéret. *Two Studies of a Seated Woman*
14 3/4 x 9 9/16" Catalogue number 97

Plate 174
Jules Chéret. *'Aimons-Nous'*
11⅛ x 14³⁄₁₆″ Catalogue number 87

Plate 175
Alphonse Legros. *Portrait of Arsène Alexandre*
14⅜ x 9⅞" Catalogue number 230

Plate 176
Henri de Toulouse-Lautrec. *Horses*
5⅞ x 9⅝″ Catalogue number 293

Plate 177
Henri de Toulouse-Lautrec.
In the Street
18¾ x 12½″
Catalogue number 294

Plate 178
Henri de Toulouse-Lautrec.
Head of a Woman
13 $\frac{11}{16}$ x 10″
Catalogue number 295

Plate 179
Henri de Toulouse-Lautrec. *At the Circus: Acrobats*
10 x 14″ Catalogue number 296

Plate 180
Henri de Toulouse-Lautrec.
At the Circus: The Dog Trainer
14 x 10″ Catalogue number 298

Plate 181
Henri de Toulouse-Lautrec. *At the Circus: 'Chocolat'*
10 x 14″ Catalogue number 297

Plate 182
Auguste Rodin. *Cambodian Dancer*
12¾ x 9¹⁵⁄₁₆″ Catalogue number 282

Plate 183
Auguste Rodin. *Nude Seen in Profile*
12¼ x 7¹⁵⁄₁₆″ Catalogue number 281

Nineteenth Century · United States

Plate 184
James Whistler. *Study for 'Weary'*
9⅝ x 6⅞″ Catalogue number 355

Plate 185
James Whistler. *Woman with a Parasol*
6³⁄₁₆ x 3 ¹¹⁄₁₆″ Catalogue number 356

Plate 186
James Whistler. *Grey and Silver: Chelsea Embankment*
5 x 8½" Catalogue number 357

HOMER 1874

Plate 188
Winslow Homer. *Feeding Time*
8¾ x 11¼" Catalogue number 337

Plate 187
Winslow Homer. *Child Seated in a Wicker Chair*
13¼ x 10" Catalogue number 332

Plate 189
Winslow Homer. *Shepherdess of Houghton Farm*
11 x 19" Catalogue number 336

Plate 190
Winslow Homer. *Summer*
8⅝ x 4¾″ Catalogue number 334

Plate 191
Winslow Homer. *Hunting for Eggs*
9¾ x 5½″ Catalogue number 333

HOMER '16

Plate 192
Winslow Homer. *Woman Peeling a Lemon*
18⅞ x 12″ Catalogue number 335

Plate 193
Winslow Homer. *Perils of the Sea*
14⅝ x 21″ Catalogue number 338

Plate 194
Winslow Homer. *Schooner at Anchor*
16 x 24¾" Catalogue number 341

Plate 195
Winslow Homer. *Fisher Girl with Net*
11⅜ x 16⅛″ Catalogue number 340

Plate 196
Winslow Homer. *Beach Scene, Tynemouth*
11½ x 19½" Catalogue number 339

Plate 197
Winslow Homer. *An October Day*
13⅞ x 19¾" Catalogue number 348

Plate 198
Winslow Homer. *Study for 'Undertow'* (*No. 2*)
5 x 7 ¹³⁄₁₆″ Catalogue number 343

Plate 199
Winslow Homer. *Study for 'Undertow'* (*No. 3*)
5 ¾ x 7 ¼″ Catalogue number 344

Plate 200
Winslow Homer. *Studies for 'Undertow'* (*Nos. 4 and 5*)
7½ x 11⅜"(overall dimensions) Catalogue numbers 345 and 346

Plate 201
Winslow Homer. *A Good Pool, Saguenay River*
9¾ x 18⅞″ Catalogue number 349

Plate 202
Winslow Homer. *Fish and Butterflies*
14½ x 20¹¹⁄₁₆″ Catalogue number 350

Plate 203
Winslow Homer. *The Osprey's Nest*
21 ½ x 13 ⅝" Catalogue number 351

15 Oct 71

Plate 204
Alexander Wyant.
In the Woods
17¼ x 13⁹⁄₁₆"
Catalogue number 35

Plate 205
Robert Blum. *The Roses of the Señor*
10 x 12¾" Catalogue number 315

Plate 206
Robert Blum. *Two Japanese Fishing Boats on Shore*
8⁷⁄₁₆ x 11¾" Catalogue number 327

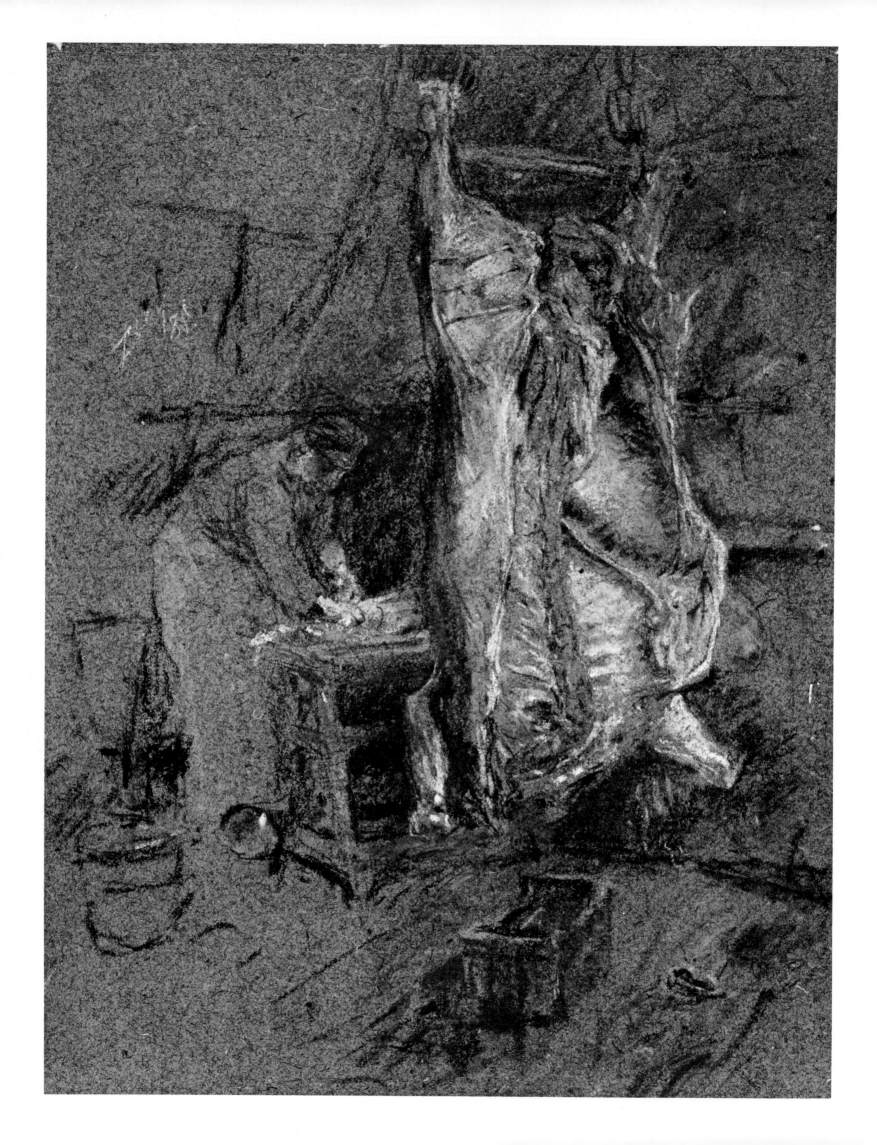

Plate 208
Robert Blum. *Two Dutch Girls Having Coffee*
12½ x 16⅟₁₆″ Catalogue number 309

Plate 207
Robert Blum. *A Slaughtered Ox in a Butcher Shop*
15 ⅓⁄₁₆ x 12¼″ Catalogue number 308

Plate 210
Robert Blum. *View of the Gulf of Corinth*
9 ¹³⁄₁₆ x 12 ¹⁵⁄₁₆″ Catalogue number 314

Plate 209
Robert Blum. *Lady Boarding a Gondola*
11 ⅞ x 9 ⁹⁄₁₆″ Catalogue number 311

Plate 211
Robert Blum. *A Street in Ikao, Japan, I*
10⅟16 x 13⅞″ Catalogue number 324

Plate 212
Robert Blum. *The Opening of the Japanese Parliament*
12⁷⁄16 x 11⅟16″ Catalogue number 319

Plate 213
Robert Blum. *Where Saké is Sold*
6⁷⁄₁₆ x 7¹³⁄₁₆″ Catalogue number 317

Plate 214
Robert Blum. *Endo Morito's Remorse*
13½ x 12⅝″ Catalogue number 318

Plate 215
Robert Blum. *A Japanese Girl*
18 x 13⅞" Catalogue number 320

F 392

Plate 216
Arthur Burdett Frost.
Br'er Rabbit
14¾ x 10¾"
Catalogue number 330

Mary Cassatt

Plate 218
Arthur Burdett Frost. *The Rialto – Broadway and Fourteenth Street*
15 x 13⅜″ Catalogue number 331

Plate 219
John Singer Sargent. *Sketch for 'Fumée d'ambre-gris'*
11⅜ x 7¹³⁄₁₆″ Catalogue number 353

Plate 217
Mary Cassatt. *Girl with Red Hat*
20¾ x 17⅛″ Catalogue number 329

Plate 220
John Singer Sargent.
Street in a Mediterranean Town
14 x 9 15/16″ Catalogue number 354

Plate 221
John La Farge. *Design for a Stained-Glass Window*
9⅛ x 5¾″ Catalogue number 352

Nineteenth Century · Various Countries

Plate 222
Mariano Fortuny. *Toreador*
10 x 7″ Catalogue number 364

Plate 223
Raimundo Madrazo. *Woman with Guitar*
19⅝ x 12¼" Catalogue number 365

Plate 224
Isidro Nonell. *Gypsies*
15¼ x 10½" Catalogue number 366

Plate 225
Anders Zorn. *'Une première'*
13 x 10¼″ Catalogue number 367

Plate 226
Anton Mauve. *A Shepherd and his Flock*
7⅞₆ x 11¾" Catalogue number 361

Plate 227
Shō tei. *Birds on a Branch*
9⅝ x 7⅝″ Catalogue number 368